TAX SEASON OPPORTUNITY GUIDE

27 Ways to
Make More Money,
Service Clients Better, and
Have More Fun
During Tax Season

With Checklists, Illustrative Examples, Sample Forms,
and Step-by-Step Instructions

By Edward Mendlowitz,
CPA, ABV, PFS

D1447345

Library Data
Mendlowitz, Edward
Tx Season Opportunity Guide
ISBN-13: 978-0-9827147-6-8
1. Accounting firms – Management. 2. Accounting firms – United States
                I. Mendlowitz, Edward, 1942-

CONTENTS

ABOUT THE AUTHOR

Edward Mendlowitz - CPA, ABV, PFS

Edward Mendlowitz is a featured contributor to CPA Trendlines (cpatrendlines.com) and a partner in Withum Smith + Brown's New Brunswick, NJ, office. He has over 40 years of public accounting experience and is a licensed certified public accountant in the states of New Jersey and New York and is accredited by the American Institute of Certified Public Accountants (AICPA) in business valuation (ABV), certified in financial forensics (CFF) and as a personal financial specialist (PFS). Ed is also admitted to practice before the United States Tax Court and has testified as an expert witness in federal and state court regarding business valuations, and twice at the House Ways and Means Committee on tax reform, fairness and reduction

A graduate of City College of New York, Ed earned his bachelor of business administration degree. He is a member of the AICPA, the New Jersey Society of Certified Public Accountants (NJSCPA) and the New York State Society of Certified Public Accountants (NYSSCPA). In addition, Ed was a founding partner of Mendlowitz Weitsen, LLP, CPAs, which merged with WS+B in 2005. Currently, he serves on the NYSSCPA Estate Planning Committee, and was chairman of the committee that planned the

NYSSCPA's 100th Anniversary. The author of 19 books, Ed has also written hundreds of articles for business and professional journals and newsletters. He is the contributing editor to the *Practitioners Publishing Company's 706/709 Deskbook*, and the *AICPA's Management of an Accounting Practice Handbook, Corporate Controller's Handbook* and *Wiley's Handbook on Budgeting* and is on the editorial board of *Bottom Line/Personal* newsletter and the *Journal of Accountancy* Member Panel on Business Valuation. Appearing regularly on television news programs, Ed has also been quoted in numerous major newspapers and periodicals in the United States. He is the recipient of the Lawler Award for the best article published during 2001 in the *Journal of Accountancy*.

Ed is a frequent speaker to many professional and business groups, including the AICPA, NJSCPA, NYSSCPA, American Management Association, the National Committee for Monetary Reform, University of Medicine and Dentistry in NJ and many more. For 11 years, he taught courses on financial analysis, corporate financial policy and theory, monetary and fiscal policy and managerial accounting in the MBA program at Fairleigh Dickinson University.

INTRODUCTION

Since 1980 I have been presenting *Managing Your Tax Season* programs for many accounting groups including the AICPA, NJSCPA, NYSSCPA and CTSCPA. I have also authored two books for the AICPA with that title. Wrote many articles for the *Journal of Accountancy* on the subject and developed and presented four webinars for Accounting Today Institute, also on the topic.

Two personal benefits of the writing and speaking is that it focuses me on what is happening, the processes, error avoidance, interaction with clients and forces me to be able to clearly relay what I see and possible solutions. The other benefit is the calls I have received from hundreds of CPAs asking questions or letting me know how they do things. In some way, I have become a clearinghouse for tax season processes and procedures.

What follows is a condensation of some major procedures and methods to better serve your clients, grow your practice and have more fun. Everything here works – whether for me, my firm or the hundreds of CPAs that shared what they do. Knowing how busy tax preparers are during that time of year I tried to be as stingy with words as possible working with bullets and brief introductions to each section. These 27 ways work. Try some, or even one – but do something and get started to making more money, servicing clients better and having more fun!

-- *Edward Mendlowitz*

12 Reasons to Love Tax Season

Tax season presents exciting opportunities for CPA firms and their staff where every moment should be enjoyed and appreciated. Following are twelve reasons:

1. Tax season is profitable and accounting is a business where we try to maximize our earnings. Sure, there is a great concentration of work in a short period with occasional pressure, but if handled properly, the work can be managed sensibly with tensions at reasonable levels. I also believe much of the pressure is self-induced by poor scheduling, inadequate quality control and the lack of uniform systems that are followed by everyone in the firm, particularly the partners.

2. The sharp concentration of work creates the need for innovation and quick training to lessen the time and workload. This presents opportunities for staff to be trained, grow and attain responsibility. It also has led firms to be innovative in using their resources and has placed accounting firms among the earliest users of PCs and laser printers to generate complete tax returns in-house and to use "cloud" software to have continuously updated tax programs that could be accessed anywhere a PC can get a signal. CPAs also were the earliest adapters of email, high speed scanners second monitors, portals and secure Internet transmission. In some respects the smaller firms led the profession in this area as they were able to make the quick acquisition decisions tax season demanded.

3. The tax preparation portion of our practices is a separate business and needs continuous product development, work efficiency improvement, and service program upgrades. It is a mini idea factory for our firms with continuous efficiency and quality control initiatives.

4. The concentration of work makes the staff well rounded and tax knowledgeable. Further, there are myriad opportunities for lower level staff to speak to clients. With most business clients the only people dealing directly with clients are the managers and partners. For individual tax preparation work it is not unusual for low level staff people to call clients to get additional data, convey information and also be the first person the client addresses questions to or expresses a financial issue that is on their mind.

5. The tax laws change on a fairly regular basis creating a level playing field for knowledge of the new tax information. The least experienced staff member can know as much about the new laws as the most experienced.

6. When you meet people who possibly can become clients, or hear you are a CPA they usually ask a tax question. Very few ask about an FASB or IFRS application.

Working on tax returns arms staff with that ammunition.

7. Taxes lead you to the best opportunities to get new clients. This can be proven by tracing the family tree of your largest clients. Many trace back to a 1040.

8. Tax season is a relationship builder. It is not unusual for a staff person to interact with a couple of dozen clients during tax season. In a professional services firm, relationships are currency.

9. Staff working late get "free" dinners.

10. Staff going home late do not have congested traffic to deal with.

11. Everyone knows about tax season, so you can get out of going to third birthday parties of your spouses' cousins in laws' kids.

12. It is fun! Many firms expend great energy hiring and adding staff and then make no effort to excite them and make them feel part of the firm afterwards. Working at this takes almost no effort and yields extremely high results. Tax season is a perfect time to foster this feeling. Instead of assigning a "list of returns" to a staff person, show them the personal benefits of working on individual tax returns and the value created for clients. For the partners, we all love the work. Those who stay in the profession past the initial few years are happy campers rarely regretting their career decision and path. Transmit those feelings!

27 Ways to Make More Money, Service Clients Better, and Have More Fun During Tax Season

1. How to be more touchy-feely with clients

Occasionally accountants lose touch with their clients especially during tax season. Part of this is because of the crush of work, which is compressed into a pretty short period. We sometimes lose sight that we are working on something the clients consider one of the most important things in their lives at that moment. Clients are not numbers on a list that needs to be reduced – they are all individuals and consider themselves very important people and want professionals that treat them accordingly. It is attitudinal and accountants must adopt that mindset and transmit that through to their culture.

Following are a few things you can do, and should do. Not only does doing these things communicate your culture, but they are all good business.

    a) Reply when you receive info by email to let the client know it was received

    b) Call or send an email when you receive info by postal mail

    c) Call with a question, and call as soon as the questions arise. Save up the questions so you don't make numerous calls, but as soon as you've worked on everything the client provided call with questions and to resolve open items

d) Call with a suggestion (even if it is for next year) such as signing up for their employer's cafeteria plan or increasing 401k to get maximum matching or consider a one person 401k (for current year). This call can be made after tax season. If it is not necessary for the preparation of the return, put it on a follow up list and then do it.

e) Call with an unexpected result. Always do this. If you do not take the time, you will still have to handle the call, except it will be when the clients call and some may even be upset. Here are a few of the situations when you show pick up the phone

f) Client will be paying more than expected

g) Receiving a refund less than expected

h) There is a first time requirement for estimated tax for current year

i) Client needs to adjust their W-4 withholdings for current year

j) Call to tell client there will be a delay in completing their returns if something unexpected came up

k) If you are doing a return for a child at the request of a client, and did not receive all the information let the client know if there will be a delay or extension and why

2. Send the bill with the return

Tax season is a business and businesses need to be paid. It is harder to justify prices when providing services rather than products. Products are usually priced before delivery while many times services are priced after delivery, i.e. performance. Many accountants price returns before they are worked on, usually basing the fee on last year, or a rate schedule. Sending a bill with the return establishes the relationship that you should be paid promptly for the work done. It shows that you run a business and also provides a courtesy to the client in that they can immediately evaluate the cost and value of what was done

   a) The quicker you bill, the quicker you are paid

   b) The highest value after you complete the work is the first time the client sees the results of your efforts – having the bill helps the client relate the service and benefits to their cost (Note: some people believe the greatest value is when the client decides he needs the service and that's usually when you are engaged. That might be the best time to set your fee)

c) Provide details of fee for added work. Do not present one amount for everything you did. If you provided additional services, list each service with an amount. If you did five additional things, list all 5 after the listing for the preparation of the return, which should be shown first. Now the client will know what they are being charged for and the relative values. Many times the additional charge is assumed by the client to be part of the basic fee, and the listing sets the client in the right direction. If you always did those services without charging, then they are right and perhaps a one-time upward fee adjustment would be in order and for those you should call the client to inform them of what *you will be doing* and how the fee will be adjusted. You need to call the client beforehand when they feel they have some control over the situation. Calling afterwards can create bad feelings and a loss of the client as well as not getting paid, and you've sunk your time and resources into that client

d) Recognize that the tax laws have dictated additional work, even if the client's situation hasn't changed that much. Some examples are more complicated reporting of capital transactions and earned income credits, greater recognition by clients to report household employees, faster and more frequent changing tax laws, more continuing education, tax return preparer registration (it doesn't cost that much and doesn't take that long, but it is one of a myriad extra "little things" that erode profits), higher software costs, children's returns in multiple states as the "infant that is done as a courtesy" grows and greater retention requirements. Also, greater scrutiny by IRS computers need more careful preparation to avoid nuisance incorrect notices, not of your doing or fault

e) If client feels fee is too high, and all explanations fail, tell them that this is how you make your living and if they can't cover their rightful share of it, they might have to look elsewhere

f) If they say they cannot pay the bill all at once, suggest they pay it in installments by providing their credit card

3. Employ team members

If you have staff, have happy cheerful helpful people. Don't surround yourself with downers and nay-sayers. Also have team players. Part of this is your firm's culture. It takes work to get people to work together and to focus on doing what it takes to service the client fully, properly and timely. Everyone working together gets it done. You need to create that atmosphere. Here are a couple of things that will help this

    a. No jerk rule. Don't employ jerks. Bad apples bring down everyone else. If you have people not carrying their weight, not growing, nor reaching forward to help each other and clients – get rid of them

    b. Watch for movement. Many times people do not really know what to do. You have to look for and notice this and then work with the staff person to perform the way they should and how you need them do

    c. Be a role model. You are a role model whether you realize it or not. Staff sees what you do. If your attitude is annoyance when a client calls at the end of a day, or when you are on your way out to lunch, or you blame the client internally when there is a mistake, or try to pass off responsibility – that is what staff see and what they will replicate. Those that understand what you are doing and don't like it will leave you so you will end up with a bunch of jerks – like yourself!

4. Have clear instructions for clients

Providing instructions of what a client needs to do must be clear enough so that the client doesn't call you to find out what to do. Sometimes taking an extra minute to lay out what the client should do can eliminate that call or indecisive moment a client might feel

a) The object of the instructions is to have the client do what you want them to do

b) Make the instructions clear and brief

c) Many times the instructions from our tax software isn't clear, or is too long, or covers multiple things that need to be done which will confuse some clients. The object is to make it as easy as possible for the client. If necessary, do not use those instructions and make up your own

d) User-friendly should be the guidepost

e) One way is to make up a single instruction sheet for each form the client needs to file

f) Another way is to send separate emails (make sure the email is secure and meets firm client confidentiality policies) for each form being provided to the client

g) If returns or forms are sent to client with short deadlines, or if the client is the type of person that will go to the post office to have it weighted and posted, place stamps with the correct postage on the envelope

h) To perform a really high class service for clients out of the country or who cannot easily do things for themselves, ask them to provide you with the signature pages of whatever authorization you need and actually mail the forms for them. This includes you putting it in the envelope

i) The point is do whatever you can to make it easy for the client to do business with you

j) The fees should be commensurate with the services you deliver to the client. If the fees aren't, and you feel it is necessary to do the extra work to properly service the client, then consider telling the client that they should consider going elsewhere

k) Make your deliverables user-friendly

5. Provide consistency in service, processes, standards

One way to guarantee extra work is to have everything always done differently each time it is done. Not establishing uniform procedures is bad business and unnecessarily consumes part of your life. Consistency in performance reduces work and review time and creates a greater reliance on the staff people

a) Establish checklists whenever repetitive procedures are to be performed. Also make sure the checklists are used. Staff need to learn that the checklists are necessary for them to do their work properly. They are not to be filled out after the work is completed as "punishment"

b) Partners, managers and reviewers are responsible for the checklist use. When they aren't used or aren't used properly, the staff needs to be told they did not do the job right and it is their responsibility to use the checklist as they do the work

c) An owner or effective manager needs to examine processes and where applicable create standardized methods

d) Standards must be consistent. Ethics, morals and courtesy are not guidelines, but the way to act in all situations

e) Be consistent

6. Eliminate atmosphere of urgency

Urgency creates stress and pressure and leads to mistakes and improper perceptions of the quality of the work

a) Planning and execution reduce urgency

b) One way to eliminate urgency is to properly plan the work with realistic deadlines and proper resources

c) Tax returns should be assigned to the proper level available staff person. Occasionally returns are given to staff with other work commitments and if there is incomplete information a break occurs and the return can't be picked up by the person that started it, causing additional delays creating urgency

d) No one likes to always work under pressure and an atmosphere of occasional urgency usually grows into perpetual urgency for everything. Playing catch up does not make happy campers

e) Clients never like to get things at the last minute. When they do it gives them an impression of disorder

f) A test of timely performance is whether the returns are sent by express mail or postal mail. When a client receives a return by FedEx or UPS it gives a last minute urgency impression. When sent by regular mail, there is no impression – it is as it should be

7. Don't be sloppy instead of thorough

All work has to be reviewed. And clients and others look at it. Sloppy work is always evident and usually incomplete. Thorough work is careful and usually complete. Thorough work takes longer when first being worked on, but review time is drastically reduced. Further sloppy work takes longer to be reviewed and longer for the preparer to be acclimated with the file when picking it up to make changes

a) All work has to be done properly and it is much smarter to do it right the first time

b) No matter how rushed you are to get something done and how much you rush to get it done, you will always have to find the time to redo it to make it right

c) Teach your staff to work deliberate and focused with the goal that there is an important reason for them to do it, and they should treat what they are doing with that importance. They owe that to the client

d) Doing it right the first time is smart business

e) You are only measured based on your last screw up

8. Stop the small leaks that can cause great damage

Some people are micro managers and anal with details. Others are big picture managers letting details take care of themselves. Neither is completely effective and both disciplines need to be balanced. There is a time for details and a time for big picture thinking. When setting up procedures and processes it is essential that all details be considered and planned for. Once the process is set up, there should be brief but continuous monitoring. And then the big picture thinking should take over – that is where you will make your money. But you can't get to the big picture ever if you are always immersed in the details. Not setting up methods right at the beginning and permitting a lack of adherence to them will thwart any chance of growth and the success you can achieve

a) Small leaks are continuous errors, inattention, lack of focus and failure to follow procedures or use checklists

b) Not catching small errors or a divergence of proper processes shows a lack of oversight that is usually taken advantage of with more and more digressions

c) If is much easier to stop small leaks than big floods

d) Errors are just that. We all make them and they need to be overlooked. What cannot be overlooked is repeated errors or a continuous lack of care or following procedures

e) Management is making sure procedures are being followed. If a procedure is not good, then change it. Otherwise, until change comes, follow it

9. Accommodate clients

Clients are our customers. They pay our salary and enable us to make good livings. Do what you can to accommodate them and make them feel important – as important as they believe they are. Also be user-friendly – do not make it difficult to work with you. Clients don't know how smart we are – they think we are great – but they measure us by the small things – the good and bad

a) Have your phones answered whenever someone is in the office

b) Do extras for them where possible

c) Call to gives a heads up on unexpected results – good as well as bad results

d) Occasionally give them an extra

e) Return their calls

f) Don't blow deadlines

g) Be available

h) When a client complains, deal with it immediately, recognize the importance of the problem to the client, and learn how to feel the way the client feels about it. You can't fool the client into thinking you care, if you don't.

10. Don't end up with a graveyard of lost opportunities

Many opportunities only come along once. The way to be successful is to not let them pass by without acting on them or taking advantage of them. Spotting opportunities is quite easy if you are looking for them – and extremely difficult if you don't have a clue of client needs or wants

a) Opportunity: something that comes up once where you can take advantage of it

b) Lost opportunities: Not acting when you should to help the client

c) An opportunity is something that comes your way for advancement or success – you need to be alert to them

d) Occasionally a one-time situation

e) Many overlooked opportunities cannot be recouped

f) Every opportunity represents additional ability to help a client, make more money and have more fun if it is a challenging situation

11. Be happy with your practice

Successful people are happy with their practices and
what they do and get joy from interacting and helping
clients. I know a lot of accountants that continuously
complain about tax season – yet they make most of
their money during the period. Do they expect
someone to knock on their door with a wheel barrel
of money to hand them? If they are financially secure,
why do they keep working? If they are not, then,
DUH! Either do it or find something else, but stop
complaining. Better yet, look at all the benefits from
what you do (If you need me to tell you the benefits
then find something else to do)

Here are two short questions to answer. If both are in
the affirmative, good for you. If one is negative, then
do something about it (actually, you are doing
something because you are reading this – so good for
you!)

43

a) I am happy with my practice, the way I work, its size and with what I earn.

Yes_____ No_____

b) I am happy with **my practice**, the **way I work**, **its size** and **with what I earn**.

Yes_____ No_____

Yes, I know the second question is the same as the first, but I highlighted the four parts, and you should be happy with each part as well as the whole. If not, then you can start concentrating on the one or two parts you are not happy with, rather than deal in an abstract feeling without any way to start making it better.

12. Recognize your resources

We have many resources and need to recognize that.
And we need to treat each with its own importance.
Even if you did everything yourself, you'd still need to
rely. Your tax software company, FedEx and the
Postal Service, stationery supplier, computer
consultant, the Internet and email, cell phone provider
and copier/scanner machine are just a few of the
resources we rely on. Managing your resources well
creates an aura of security and consistency to your
practice.

Here are some more resources that need to be
managed:

a) Staff

"I know what I mean" is a common thought when
people tell others what to do. But, does the person
who is going to do the work know what you mean?
When you have people working for you it is important
they know what to do. Your instructions must be
clear enough for them to be able to do what you want
them to do.

Systems, processes, checklists and training are other
ways to manage staff and control what they do and
how they do it. So does oversight, review and quality
control procedures

b) Quality of clients

Having good clients is important. Nasty or mean spirited or unhappy clients determine the pulse of how your practice breathes. The type of clients also creates feelings. Good clients = good feelings. Bad clients = bad feelings.

You spend plenty of time at work – shouldn't it be done with nice people?

c) Suppliers

Suppliers are your partners. Treat them courteous. You are their clients – act the way you want your clients to act with you. Some suppliers are more of a partner than others. The people that respond and repair your hardware or software are more valuable to you than the paper supplier, so treat them in that regard. You having a bad day doesn't mean you should try to see that those interacting with you also have a bad day

d) Partners

Have the right people as partners. Partners are joint owners in your income production. It is important to be in sync and to share each other's thoughts on essential practice, staff and client management issues. Arrange regular time to talk about the business – don't get so caught up working *in* the business that you lose sight of working *on* the business. Tax season is a period where serious discussion time needs to be scheduled and spent and I suggest doing it out of the office. So much is happening so quickly that some time needs to be spent catching your breath and discussing what is going on. An hour and a half to two hours set aside every other week will not cause any practice to cease production, but can be a great pick-me-up

e) Family

Your spouse and children are resources. If you don't think so, what happens when you need to work on something extremely critical on a weekend or late and cannot attend a planned family event? How they react can set a tone for how you feel about doing what you need to do.

The family of your staff likewise are partners in your endeavors. If staff goes home upset and transmits that feeling, you have people you don't know and can't control telling your "valuable" staff person that maybe it is time to look elsewhere. Contrarily, if you can contribute to making the family feel good you will have a chorus singing praises about you. Some things you can do is pay well, make sure your staff go home happy at night, make sure they are excited about what they learn and do, occasionally send flowers or plants to the spouse or partner of a staff person thanking them for "loaning" them to you, spring for a gift card for dinner at a fancy restaurant or get theatre or sports tickets, give a floating day to take off for a family event, or have summer family picnics.

f) Friends

True friends you can share thoughts, let off steam, act yourself and not have to be "on," or just have fun with are an important resource, if for nothing else than your mental health

g) Referrers of business

These are valuable resources and they need to be made to feel appreciated. Sometimes it is another professional that does the referring and it is difficult at best to be able to reciprocate. Tell them you appreciate what they do. Send them an occasional gift – not an expensive one, but something that shows you care. An example is to get an attorney a framed limited edition print of the signing of the U.S. Constitution, an autograph of a Supreme Court Justice they seem to like, an old law book or patent or Presidential commission. You can also try to get them autographed copies of a new book written by a famous jurist or attorney. Use your ingenuity to come up with something – the important thing is to show you care about them

h) Your office

The physical space is important. Room to work quietly, meet with clients, interact with partners and staff, and spread out allows work to proceed efficiently and get done the way it should when it should.

Messy surroundings and desks make it harder to work, and convey feelings that you are not in control. It also condones messiness. I once saw a sign on a messy desk that said: If a messy desk is a sign or a messy mind, what is an empty desk a sign of?

Many people have meetings in sterile conference rooms, so don't need to keep their desks neat should a client drop in. However, your other constituencies see it – partners, staff, family, friends and suppliers

i) Office decoration or conference room

Conference rooms either do not show off a personality or show one that is corporate. Your individual office should reflect your interests and personality. I like seeing people's offices – it is a small window to who they are. One or two prints on the wall, a statue, or book lying around can tell a lot about who they are. Further, not seeing anything personal can also tell you who they are. What about an office with no books?

13. Quick and easy research

I keep a few of the one volume tax guides in my office so I could look up a quick answer when I need to. Recently a golf buddy emailed me a question that I thought I could answer quickly. He wanted to know that if he was in the "zero" percent capital gains tax bracket, did that apply to an unlimited amount of capital gains? Sounds like a simple question. Well I looked it up on line and then in three one volume tax guides. Only one source had thorough coverage of the issue. I ended up spending an hour on this "simple" question including my emailed response. Nothing is simple anymore

a) Research techniques

Needing an answer to a question you don't know will slow you up and insert a bottleneck in your production line. There are three types of research – light, heavy and just want to make sure. Every preparer should be equipped with a one volume tax guide (either paper or a digital version) to look up questions. My rule is simple. If a preparer doesn't know something – they should spend a half hour, but not any more time than that and if they don't have an answer, they should go to someone above them for assistance. Show them what you found or did not find and ask how you should proceed. Sometimes they will point them in the right direction, and sometimes it would be something above their level and they will get the answer. The first person trying to find the answer is what I call light research. Heavy research is where the higher level person says they will find the answer. This requires additional work, skills and resources that they are more competent to do or have. Many times you know something, but just want to make sure – that is a minute or two project and should be done by anyone feeling that way

b) Don't let not having an immediate answer slow up the return

Not having an immediate answer to a question does not mean work should stop. Work around it getting everything else completed so when that response is received, the return can be easily completed. Every return should have an open item listing. The issue needing heavy research should be the only entry on that list. Stopping work leaves a larger volume of work undone and it will make it harder for someone else to pick up on the return should the original preparer not be available to complete the return

c) Stopping slows up the momentum

Each client's return is treated special but the work load requires a method similar to an assembly line, and any slow up reduces the momentum. Because of this, it is important to have a minimum number of stoppages. This can be accomplished by as much as possible being done each time there is a "touch" while at the same time reducing the number of touches. As much as possible needs to be done each time the return is worked on with nothing left for later. When a question needs research, it should be done immediately within the half hour rule expressed above. Anything not resolved creates delay and increases the time to complete the return

d) Putting something aside creates a "mortgage" of work that will still need to be done – it won't go away

All returns will need to be completed and at some point, there is no tomorrow. A no tomorrow attitude will reduce delays and time needed to work on a return. Anything pushed forward will become a mortgage on that return increasing the time to get it completed and pushing forward the completion date

14. Fix the top 21 reasons why clients switch firms

Clients have many choices including the choice of a tax preparer. Every new client an accountant gets is because that client left – fired – their previous accountant. Following is a listing of major reasons why clients switch accountants

1) Owed a large amount that wasn't expected

2) Get super large refund that wasn't expected

3) Doesn't return phone calls

4) Last minute rush

5) Errors every year

6) Large (or even a small) error not apologized for, or explained

7) "Dumb" phone calls from CPA's office

8) Fee too high (based on previous years)

9) Got notice and paid penalty that was preparers fault

10) Paid interest on a late payment that was caused by CPAs delay

11) Accountant didn't follow up on something they should have

12) CPA should have called me more frequently for missing info

13) I was charged for a redo for a corrected statement from my broker

14) I was charged for handling a notice that was erroneously sent to me by IRS

15) I was billed for people working on return that I never heard of

16) Billed for staff people correcting errors they made (this was said on the time run sent to me with bill)

17) CPA lost personal touch

18) Person handling my account left and was not comfortable with new person

19) Practice was sold and I never heard from new accountant

20) CPAs appearance and office looked out of control

21) Don't see CPA as a "partner"

15. Eliminate excuses

Tax season is a busy time and preparers some time neglect to get something outside of tax prep done. Here are a bunch of phony reasons why something did not get done

a) Too busy (during tax season – 3+ months)

b) Not my job

c) I called them last; it's their turn to call me

d) Too hard

e) Too new

f) Not sure I could do it

g) Won't get credit

h) It "smells" so don't try – should ask "how we can make it happen" rather than discuss why "it won't work"

i) I need a new computer

j) Always too busy and seem to be playing catch up

Some firms have a 3-plus month tax season where the owners work 80 or more hours a week. Each of the above reasons are valid at one time or another, but to the client, his work is super important and the above reasons will not assuage them

16. Think like an entrepreneur

Accountants and tax practitioners are entrepreneurs. This means their practice needs to be run as a business with sound business decisions being made. These decisions need to be made in the context of growing the business, adding processes and controls and making greater profit

a) Do you consider yourself an entrepreneur?

Yes_____   No_____

b) If you are a sole practitioner or partner, do you consider yourself an entrepreneur?

Yes_____   No_____

c) Under what circumstances would you do a tax return for $190?

_____

_____

Those that responded "no" to this question need to look at the next question and then see my comment and suggestions regarding $190 tax returns, and then re-answer this question.

17. Consider some H&R Block statistics

H&R Block is a tax preparation business - a big business, but nevertheless the same business as we are. Let's look at their numbers

a) In 2011 H&R Block did 9,168,000 tax returns for that average fee - $190

b) In 2010 they did 9,182,000 returns for $197

c) 2009 10,231,000 for $196

d) 2003   9,995,000 for $138

e) 2002 10,431,000 for $130

f) 2001 10,275,000 for $118

$190 tax returns

a) Suppose you had an opportunity to do 400 tax returns at that fee.

b) That's $76,000 revenue.

c) Tax returns each took 1½ hours total time.

d) 600 hours over a 3 month period.

e) That's 50 12 hour days.

f) Average per hour = $127

g) Suppose return takes 1 hour each

h) Average per hour = $190

i) Suppose staff does 90% of the work?

Different observation. Their fee increased from 2001 to 2011 from $118 to $190. That is a hefty percentage – 60%. Did your fees increase that percentage over that period? They seem to have hit a wall in 2010 and 2011 where there wasn't any increase.

However there was a big jump previously. Question: Did tax preparation get more complicated during that period causing increased time, or is the fee increase simply the result of fees keeping up with inflation?

Now re-answer the questions:

a) Do you consider yourself an entrepreneur?

Yes_____   No_____

b) If you are a sole practitioner or partner, do you consider yourself an entrepreneur?

Yes_____   No_____

c) Under what circumstances would you do a tax return for $190?

18. Imagine starting with a clean slate

We all get caught up with what we do. Sometimes so much that we lose sight of what we are doing and the purpose. Also, work happens. Many of us start out with lofty plans that go astray as the practice develops. Many things cause it – clients we get, availability or lack of availability of the right staff, how we choose to learn or not learn new things, and even where we locate. Now stop for a moment, forget about what you are doing and fantasize about how you would start a practice from scratch

If you were starting out today in a tax preparation practice, what would you do?

Write out a few notes and then compare to what you have today.

_____

_____

_____

_____

Is it what you wanted? Is it what you want?

What changes would you make? What would you do
different?

Would you replicate exactly what you have right now?
If yes, then you are truly lucky.

Would you encourage your daughter to become a
CPA/tax preparer?

19. Two questions to ask yourself

1. Why should clients use you?

_____

_____

_____

2. Why should staff want to work for you?

_____

_____

_____

You should be clear on the responses to the above two questions. If you can't clearly articulate the reasons clients should use you and why staff would want to work for you, then why should they?

Some suggested responses:

1. Clients using me get a personalized service from someone that really cares, who thinks about them and looks for ways to save them taxes and make them feel more financially secure, at fees that are appropriate for what we do and the value we provide to them.

2. Staff should want to work for us because we pay reasonable salaries and overtime, won't make them come to the office to fill in time if there is no sufficient client work for them, we will train them so they can be credible members of our profession and future leaders, have them interact with clients and present them with interesting and exciting clients and services for those clients.

20. Think about the future of the tax preparation business

Industry statistics

a) Tax returns filed: In 2009, 144,000,000. In 2010, 142,000,000

b) Total E-filed: 2009, 95,500,000. 2010 98,700,000

c) E-filed: Self prepared: 2009, 32,200,000. 2010, 34,900,000

d) E-filed: Professional preparers, 2009, 63,300,000. 2010, 63,900,000

e) Visits to www.irs.gov: 2009, 290,000,000. 2010, 297,000,000

In 5 years the IRS will be able to "prepare" returns for taxpayers based on information statements submitted to them.

Professional services statistics

Industry statistics do not reflect personal care, efforts and interest many professional offer as well as decision making ability to apply the complicated tax laws to each client's individual situation. Filling in a form is not a professional service. Knowing how to plan and help clients take advantage of the tax laws is a professional service.

21. Now think about the future of your business

Do you have an opinion on the future of your business? You should. How do you think it will be in 5, 10 and 20 years?

a) 5 Years

_____

_____

_____

b) 10 Years

_____

_____

_____

c) 20 Years

_____

_____

_____

Who knows? But I don't think it will be the same as it is now.

What would your response had been if asked this question 20 years ago?

How has it changed from 20 years ago? How has your tax prep practice changed from 20 years ago?

_____

_____

_____

22. Your new marketing plan

Marketing takes many forms. Further, many accountants are not trained in marketing. I also know that while most CPAs want more business, they are too busy with what they have to be actively seeking new business. Additionally, marketing can be external, internal or retentive.

External is where new clients are solicited. That takes effort, ingenuity, time and maybe even some money.

Internal is where you sell additional services to existing clients. It takes little effort, little time and no money – but some ingenuity. It is low hanging fruit and not only can help you earn additional revenue but you will be doing a service for your clients who you will be helping become more secure in their finances.

Retentive marketing is what you do to retain or keep your clients. Almost no effort or thought other than calling an extra time during the year or dropping them a note asking how they are.

Here are some examples for a typical marketing plan:

a) Let every tax client you meet with know that you do personal financial planning (such as help with investing their 401k or IRA rollover acct, education funding planning or retirement planning)

b) Find out one thing that you could help a tax client with, and then call that client in June, July or August to come in for a paid consultation

c) Ask each tax client for a referral

d) Call every tax client at least once after July 1 to see how they are doing and if you could assist them in any way

Now, write out three things you could do as part of
your marketing plan

1.

_____

_____

2.

_____

_____

3.

_____

_____

23. Know your value

Know your value to your clients. Better, understand your business and what you really do and what you add to the client's life.

I had a group of gastroenterologists as clients that were going to get into a business of inserting a Gastric Bubble into people's stomachs. There were a number of issues to this.

It was an operation – operations are only minor when it is not you. When the Gastric Bubble was in their stomach it was blown up so their stomach would feel full and they would not "want to eat more", and they would then lose weight. Sounds good – so far.

As part of the process they told me a nutritionist was essential for behavior modification. They said that the patient wasn't going to lose weight unless they changed their eating habits -- what they ate, when they ate, and how much they ate. They had to really, really, really want to lose weight – nothing else replaced that.

Question: How necessary was the Gastric Bubble? Did the Bubble add value or was it a method of getting them to the nutritionist?

What is your method to help your clients?

    a) What help do they need?

    b) Is the only thing you can do for your clients is a tax return or are there any other services they need that you can do, or should do?

    c) Does what you do need a "nutritionist" or is the service the entire thing they need done by you?

24. Know yourself

Is your practice satisfying? Do you like it the way it is, or do you want it to develop and grow? Some people like the way things are and don't care about change. If you've gotten this far, I would suggest that you do care about change, and change means you have to do some things differently. Nothing different means no change

a) A family person

b) An involved member of a religion

c) An accountant

d) A business advisor

e) A problem solver

f) Someone just traveling through trying not to leave any footprints

g) Decide which you are and work accordingly. Place your greater importance on the type of person that you are that is most important to you

25. What's needed for growth and success

All these elements are essential:

a) Services innovation

b) Culture of excellence

c) Technology

d) Mindset to succeed

e) Focus on your goals

f) Clients

g) Great client service

h) The right staff

i) Effective training

Each one that is not present diminishes your practice.

Next: Rate yourself on each element and set up a plan of what you will do, and when you will start.

Element	I'm on target	I need to work on this	What I am going to do	When I will start
Services innovation				
Culture of excellence				
Technology				
Mindset to succeed				
Focus on your goals				
Clients				
Great client service				
The right staff				
Effective training				

26. Know your tax practice metrics

On the next page, try filling in your numbers. See if there is growth, stagnation or decline. Think back to when you started. How rapid was the growth? Compare that to now.

Metrics	2013 expected	2012 actual	2011 actual	2010 actual
# 1040 only clients				
% increase (decrease) from prior year				
Are you ☺ or ☹				
# new 1040 clients				
% increase (decrease) from prior year				
Are you ☺ or ☹				
Total fees from 10 largest 1040 clients you had this period				
% increase (decrease) from prior year				
Are you ☺ or ☹				
Total fees from 10 smallest 1040 clients you had this period				
% increase (decrease) from prior year				
Are you ☺ or ☹				
Total fees from all 1040s (including 1040s for business clients)				
% increase (decrease) from prior year				
Are you ☺ or ☹				

27. You are the artist

It is your practice. It is your canvas. Paint on it as you wish

  a) Like and admire your painting

  b) Be a continuous re-toucher

  c) Don't be afraid to restart

  d) Are you unaware of yourself as an artist?

Doing *anything* discussed in this book, results in:

  a) **You** providing better service to clients

  b) **You** making more money

  c) **You** having more fun

BONUS APPENDIX

Top 12 Tax Return Preparation Errors

1. Number transposition and spelling errors. This includes income and deduction amounts and client Social Security numbers, addresses and zip codes. Spelling errors should also be avoided – they indicate a lack of attention to what you are doing.

2. Unreported 1099 income. Clients frequently leave out 1099s, but the preparer should make sure all 1099 items from last year are accounted for. Missing 1099s that were not final for last year should be accounted for.

3. Tax payments. Entering incorrect and unpaid amounts can be avoided by requiring the client to provide "proof" of the payments. Entering "incorrect" amounts provided by the client is a major cause of tax notices.

4. Keeping review notes after the return is completed. This can create liability issues if there is ever a controversy over the return. Review notes usually deal with errors and omissions and the type and quantity of them can indicate a lack of training, proper procedures, adherence to processes or care. Retaining these notes cannot ever help you.

5. Not correcting reason for tax notices for prior year on this year's return. This is a no brainer, but for many preparers there is a disconnect between a notice for last year's return and the preparing of this year's return.

6. Not questioning numbers that stretch the imagination. My imagination is likely to be different from yours, but a client with high debt indicated by mortgage and home equity loan interest usually won't be making cash charitable contributions equal to 8 percent of their gross income. Likewise for maximum allowable IRA contributions. Explain the requirements for substantiating these deductions and ask client if they have it.

7. Not following up enough with clients to get missing information. This could create last minute rushes and unhappy clients, even though it was because of client's lack of response.

8. Not specifically asking clients if they have, can sign or control a foreign bank account

9. Not telling client about items that aren't on return. Items such as traditional and Roth IRAs, SEPs, making charitable contributions with appreciated stock, claiming a grown child with minimal income who lives with client as a dependent, or signing up for an employer's 401k plan and/or flexible spending account, or partial exercising of ISOs to avoid AMT.

10. High mortgage interest deductions. Excessive amounts (usually over $50,000) are a red flag for the IRS. Make sure the interest is not from excessive mortgages, that the funds were used for proper purposes or that the interest tracking rules have been complied with and if mortgage proceeds were used for investment purposes, it is properly reflected on the return.

11. Alternative minimum tax. Watch for unapplied AMT credits and AMT NOLs, and state tax refunds reported as income even though not deducted in prior year because of AMT.

12. Not calling a client to relay unexpected (and especially bad) final results

Checklist for What Makes a Good Tax Season Client

Clients are our customers that pay our salaries and present us with stimulating opportunities allowing us to grow. There is no such thing as a bad or nuisance client, although there are clients that sometimes do bad or nuisance things.

Following is a listing of what makes a good client.

1. Clients that do what they say they will do and who do not delay sending us what we ask for

2. Clients that do the work organizing their documents before they provide it to us

3. Clients that give us estimated amounts that tell us they are estimates and how they arrived at it and why they cannot provide the actual amounts

4. Clients that pay their bills promptly

5. Clients that call the partner to complain about a bill instead of "complaining" by sending a note to our "bookkeeping department"

6. Clients that complain right away to the partner when they are upset with something, and not to a staff person who happens to be at their office at that moment

7. Clients that make us explain clearly what we tell them to do, and who don't give the go ahead without fully understanding what is to be done

8. Clients who review the work we send them when it is received and who don't sit on it until eight minutes before it needs to be filed or sent to a bank

9. Clients that use technology fully

10. Clients that are not litigious

11. Clients that understand that taxes need to be paid to maintain our society and that we do not make the rules that cause them to pay taxes

12. Clients that realize that banks and finance companies need back up and documentation when they lend funds, and that there is a cost to develop that data, and that it is not our "fault" the work is needed

13. Clients that understand that we sometimes make a mistake, who accept a rational and reasonable

explanation and who won't keep bringing it up months and years later

14. Clients that occasionally thank us for our efforts on their behalf

15. Clients that refer potential clients

16. Clients who are happy with their lives

Reviewer's Checklist For Individual Tax Returns

Client _____ **Year** _____

Date Prepared By _____ **Date** _____

Following is a suggested checklist of things for the reviewer to do:

1. ___ Review client's name and address, Social Security numbers and business code (if applicable) (if this is first year doing this client's return)

2. ___ Review Excel tax comparison worksheet – current and prior year's summary information, and projection if one was prepared, and explanations for large variances, differences, inconsistent amounts, and surprise items

3. ___ Compare last year's return with this year's return if Excel worksheet was not prepared

4. ___ Were last year's unusual or large items reviewed to see if they were applicable for this year

5. ___ Verify that estimated tax payments were made

6. ___ Review that estimated tax payments were entered properly on Tax Payments Worksheet

7. ___ Review that estimated payments were calculated properly for the current year

8. ___ Review K-1 input

9. ___ Review W-2 input

10. ___ Total of all 1099s should tie in with amounts on return

11. ___ Were carryforwards entered properly and accounted for

12. ___ Were suspended losses properly treated

13. ___ Were gross sales from security transactions reconciled with 1099s (we have form for this)

14. ___ Review cost basis on 1099s and return for wash sales, gifted and inherited stocks

15. ___ Compare federal to state returns to see that add backs and reductions seem logical

16. ___ If a trial balance or financial statement was provided for client's Schedule C business, reconcile any book to tax differences or adjustments, and that they appear reasonable

17. ___ Were items on flag sheets, notes based on discussions with client during the year, special instructions and knowledge points in tax control considered

18. ___ Look at client's correspondence and notes that accompanied tax information to see if applicable to the tax return preparation or if it requires separate follow up actions

19. ___ Address any notes or comments by a partner

20. ___ Look at tax notices for last year to see if they affect current year's return

21. ___ Should be no diagnostics, open or unresolved items

22. ___ Were all questions on the preparer's checklist answered. Should be no unanswered items

23. ___ Address S Corporation distributions to client in excess of AAA or with negative capital

24. ____ If self-employment income, was a SEP or other pension plan payment made or considered

25. ____ If client did not make maximum IRA contributions, were they made aware of it

26. ____ Was question for foreign bank accounts or signatory powers checked and Form TDF 90-22.1 prepared if required.

27. ____ If not checked, was client asked if they had a foreign account or signatory powers:

____Yes, ____No
(If no, make sure they are asked question)

28. ____ Review AMT adjustments, calculations and opportunities to use AMT credit from prior years

29. ____ Are filing and estimated tax instructions correct

30. ____ All penalties, interest, underpayment and late filing penalties should be calculated

31. ____ Look at every page of completed return and review for any obvious red flags or audit triggers

32. ____ Was there any follow through by client on tax or financial planning recommendations made last year.

33. Report any comments:

a. _____

b. _____

c. _____

d. _____

34. ____ Were opportunities identified for tax or financial planning for the client. This should be followed up after tax season. Put on tax calendar with date. If not included on separate checklist, list here:

a. _____

b. _____

c. _____

d. _____

Reviewer's Checklist For Business Tax Returns

Client _____ **Year** _____

Prepared By _____ **Date** _____

[Notes: 1) The term owners will be used to refer to stockholders, partners or members, as the case may be. 2) Even though "trial balance" is used in this check list, you can use the Company's financial statements if that was what was used for the preparation of the tax return, or computer generated statements]

Following is a suggested checklist of things for the reviewer to do:

1. ____ Did audit manager of this client review the input and result Yes____ No____

2. ____ Review client's name and address, business code, State of incorporation and all EINs and owner's Social Security numbers (if this is first year doing this client's return)

3. ____ Pass through entities: managing owner should have submitted an updated address list

    through entities with change

in ownership: verify that the dates of change and income allocations were entered and allocated properly

5. ___ For first year, make sure all the proper elections have been made such as accounting basis, inventory method, Section 263A, S elections (including State), mark to market for traders, depreciation and amortization. For later years make sure return is consistent with elections

6. ___ Make sure all questions on return have been answered

7. ___ Determine that accounting basis listed on the tax return is consistent with the income statement and balance sheet presentation on tax return (for example, if the cash basis is checked, make sure the balance sheet on the tax return is prepared using the cash basis; and that there are no bad debts or inventory for a cash basis company)

8. ___ Tie in retained earnings or capital accounts balances with trial balances and tax return

9. ___ Make sure the time spent by officers is reflected as a percentage and not as "all" or "part"

10. ___ Review book to tax adjustment reconciliation and tie in totals to trial balance

11. ___ If financial statement was prepared, look at note regarding income taxes for inconsistencies

12. ___ Determine that the individual amounts on book to tax reconciliation appear reasonable

13. ___ Check that cash balance on tax return agrees with year end bank reconciliations

14. ___ Check that totals of fixed assets and accumulated depreciation and amortization on balance sheet of tax return agrees with depreciation and amortization schedules

15. ___ Verify that gross payroll on tax return agrees with gross payroll on W-3

16. ___ Tie in total of all 1099s company prepared with amounts on return

17. ___ Reconcile sales on the client's sales tax returns with the sales on the income tax return

18. ___ If company is on accrual basis, were accruals timely paid after year end

19. ___ Determine if pension accruals were properly calculated and timely and properly paid

20. ___ Was interest properly paid, received, or accrued on loans to/from related parties

21. ___ Obtain explanations for large variances, differences, inconsistent amounts, and surprise items appearing on tax return as compared to prior year and/or projections if prepared

22. ___ Were estimated tax payments entered properly on Tax Payments Worksheet

23. ___ Were estimated payments calculated properly for the current year (If a C Corp and earnings over $1,000,000 any one of last three years, different estimated tax payment rules apply)

24. ___ Are there unreasonable compensation or unreasonable accumulation of earnings issues

25. ___ Review K-1 input and tie in to distributions and investments during the year per the books

26. ___ Were carry-forwards entered properly and accounted for

27. ___ Were gross sales from security transactions reconciled with 1099s (we have form for this)

28. ___ Compare federal to state returns to see that add backs and reductions seem logical

29. ___ Address S Corporations that had distributions in excess of AAA or with negative capital

30. ___ Were there foreign relationships, transactions or ownership which require special forms such as 8804, 5471, 5472 or TDF 90-22.1

31. ___ Were items on flag sheets, notes based on discussions with client during the year, special instructions and knowledge points in tax control considered

32. ___ Look at client's correspondence and notes that accompanied tax information to see if applicable to the tax return preparation or if it requires separate follow up actions

33. ___ Address any notes or comments by a partner

34. ___ Look at tax notices for last year to see if they affect current year's return

35. ____ Should be no diagnostics, open or unresolved items

36. ____ Were all questions on the preparer's checklist answered. Should be no unanswered items

37. ____ Are filing and estimated tax instructions correct

38. ____ All penalties, interest, underpayment and late filing penalties should be calculated

39. ____ Look at every page of completed return and review for any obvious red flags or audit triggers

40. ____ Was there any follow through by client on tax or planning recommendations made last year.

Report any comments:

a. _____

b. _____

c. _____

41. ___ Were opportunities identified for tax or planning for the client? This should be followed up after tax season. Put on tax calendar with date.

List here:

a. _____

b. _____

c. _____

d. _____

Reviewer Qualification Test: 10 Questions

The primary people that should review tax returns are trained tax department reviewers. However, often the bunching and compression of work shifts some of the review to higher level non tax personnel such as audit managers and partners who might not necessarily have the comprehensive training, background, and experience to handle everything that might come up during the tax preparation process. Additionally, in many firms, almost everyone on the staff prepares some returns, and that lack of dedicated preparers with the trained skills places an added burden on the tax reviewers, making it important for them to have the range of experience needed to perform the review.

Following are 10 questions reviewers should be able to answer to qualify for their role.

Note: Whether or not you agree with the questions below, you have to consider a method for making sure reviewers are qualified. Doing so should also include reviewer-appropriate CPE and in-house training.

1. What is the latest date a simplified employer pension (SEP) plan can be opened for 2011 for a sole proprietor?

2. What date is used as the "date purchased" to report a stock transaction that includes an unallowed loss because there was a previous wash sale?

3. Are extra payments made to an ex-spouse to cover unanticipated increases in tuition in her nursing school deductible as alimony?

4. What is the maximum federal capital gains tax rate from any portion of the gain on commercial real estate that an individual tax client sells?

5. When would you use the annualization exception for the 2210 penalty?

6. How are individuals taxed on section 1256 gains?

7. How would you advise a client who makes large amounts of annual charitable contributions and typically reports large long-term capital gains?

8. What cost basis is used when a client sells at the point of vesting employer-issued restricted stock shares that had no cost and the stockbroker has provided a 1099-B showing proceeds of $8,100?

9. What would a minimum strategy be for a client with incentive stock options to avoid or partially avoid the alternative minimum tax (AMT)?

10. What is the equivalent taxable interest amount for a client with 4% municipal bond interest if his or her marginal federal tax rate is 25% (assume no state tax)?

Reviewer Qualification Test: Answers (No Peeking)

1. It can be opened through the latest due date, including extensions, of the tax return for the year 2011.

2. The date the first or original lot of stocks was purchased.

3. Voluntary payments to an ex-spouse are not deductible as alimony.

4. Pre-1987 recaptured depreciation on real estate is taxed at ordinary income rates; 1987 or later recaptured depreciation on real estate is taxed, for 2011 tax reporting, at a top capital gains rate of 25%.

5. When the income or deductions are earned erratically, bunched or not received or paid equally during the year, and it results in a lower or no 2210 penalty.

6. The gains are taxed as 60% long-term capital gains and 40% short-term capital gains regardless of holding period.

7. To consider donating appreciated long-term-held securities. The client would get a charitable deduction for the fair market value of the securities and not have to report the capital gain income.

8. The employer is required to report the entire gain as wages on the employee's Form W-2. I would use $8,100. However, the technically correct answer is the cost should be the fair market value on the date vested, before deduction for the broker's commission. A practical solution on small transactions is to use the net proceeds.

9. To consider exercising as much of the ISOs as the client can to the point where the

AMT would kick in.

10. 5.33%. Divide 4% by 75% $(1 - 25\%)$.

40 Other Services Your Tax Clients Should Know About

The following listing can give you ideas of additional services clients might need.

1. Estate planning

2. Inheritance advice and guidance

3. Succession planning

4. Personal financial planning

5. Investment allocation construction

6. Investment management

7. Investment clubs

8. Elder care assurance services

9. Business performance measurement services

10. QuickBooks® training and consulting

11. Outsource business and back office services

12. Outsourced CFO services

13. Outsourced corporate tax preparation – income taxes, executive tax preparation, sales taxes, state registrations

14. Second opinions

15. Business valuations

16. Retirement planning and counseling

17. Pension planning

18. IRA distribution analysis

19. IRS tax audit protection service

20. Conflict resolution

21. Single couples living together planning

22. Second marriage assistance

23. Pre-nuptial agreement analysis

24. Divorce settlement planning

25. Conflict resolution

26. Buying and selling a business assistance

27. Starting a business

28. Buying a franchise

29. Entering a partnership

30. Getting stock in a corporation

31. Receiving stock options

32. Projecting financial aspects of proposed actions

33. Basis calculations for pass through activities

34. Employment contract negotiations

35. Executive compensation review

36. Downsize settlement structuring

37. Corporate management and financial planning training

38. Industry specific tax and business advisory services

39. Structuring partnership and buy sell agreements

40. Recession consulting

This list is not complete, but it is a good start for you to start thinking about what types of additional services you can offer to your clients!

Checklist for Considering Additional Client Services

Client _____ **Date** _____

Prepared by _____

The following items that the client might need were identified at our meeting.

1. ____ Review adequacy of life insurance based on our discussion of family's financial needs

2. ____ Client indicated they do not have a will. We can consult on what should be in the will

3. ____ If client has a concern about their estate plan, we can advise them based on their desires

4. ____ Client said they do not have a buy-sell agreement with their business partners. We can consult on the terms that should be in the agreement and ways to value the business

5. ____ Client expressed goals of when they want to retire. We can help them develop a financial plan leading them toward achieving these goals

6. ___ Client indicated a concern about cash flow in retirement. We can review their present assets and accumulation plans to illustrate if they can achieve the targeted cash flow

7. ___ Client needs a separate tax planning consultation

8. ___ Client is subject to Alternative Minimum Tax. Client should schedule a pre year-end meeting

9. ___ Client should have a pre year-end tax planning meeting and projection

10. ___ Client indicated that they might have a big change in their income this year. Client should call us when it appears it will occur – *before* the event takes place

11. ___ Client's estimated tax payments do not protect them from penalty. Client needs to inform us before each payment is due so we could calculate protective estimated payments. Note: Due dates are June 15, September 15 and January 15 of current year.

12. ___ Client is going through a marital separation. Client should schedule an appointment to discuss the financial and tax

aspects of the separation, and possible divorce, and valuation of businesses, if any

13. ___ Client should consider a retirement plan for their business and should call for a consultation

14. ___ Client has a household employee and needs further information

15. ___ Client makes large charitable contributions and needs a consultation on tax advantaged ways to make them

16. ___ Other

    a. _____

    b. _____

    c. _____

We assume no responsibility to perform these services. Consultations are available for additional fees. Please call our office to schedule a meeting.

Tax Season Follow Up Sheet

BASED ON ISSUES DISCLOSED BY PREPARER OR REVIEWER

Client _____ **Year** _____

Prepared By _____ **Date** _____

Date followed up _____ Comments _____

_____

Date followed up _____ Comments _____

_____

Date followed up _____ Comments _____

_____

1. Issue(s) discussed:

a. _____

b. _____

c. _____

2. Follow up action:

a. _____

b. _____

c. _____

3. Client comments:

a. _____

b. _____

c. _____

FINAL RESOLUTION

4. Additional services performed:

a. _____

b. _____

c. _____

5. Future follow up date:

_____

6. Client has no interest in corrective or preventative actions: _____

7. Comments:

a. _____

b. _____

CONTACT THE AUTHOR

Ed Mendlowitz welcomes calls asking questions, looking for guidance, or offering comments or suggestions, at 732 964-9329 or email emendlowitz@withum.com

ABOUT THE PUBLISHER

Bay Street Group LLC provides custom research, marketing, communications, strategic consulting, publishing and digital media for the professional tax, accounting and finance community.

Delivering state of the art services:
- Research
- Analysis
- Communications
- Strategic Planning
- Lead Generation
- Alliances
- Business Development

With know-how and resources:
- Experience
- Insight
- Execution

PO Box 5139
East Hampton, NY 11937
Phone: (631) 604-1651

MORE FROM CPA TRENDLINES

Tax, accounting and finance professionals can find more professional resources and actionable intelligence at cpatrendlines.com, published by Bay Street Group LLC.

CPA Trendlines is the home of many practical resources, including:

- CPA Firm Management & Governance
- CPA Firm Succession Planning: A Perfect Storm
- Effective Partner Relations and Communications
- Guide to Planning the Firm Retreat
- How To Bring in New Partners
- How to Operate a Compensation Committee
- Professional Services Marketing 3.0 by Bruce W. Marcus
- Strategic Planning and Goal Setting for Results
- The Rosenberg MAP Survey
- Trends in Accounting Firm Marketing Strategies
- What Really Makes CPA Firms Profitable?

All are available at baystreetgroup.com/store.

19447896R00076

Made in the USA
Charleston, SC
24 May 2013